MANIFESTOS FOR THE 21ST CENTURY

SERIES EDITORS: URSULA OWEN AND JUDITH VIDAL-HALL

Free expression is as high on the agenda as it
has ever been, though not always for the
happiest of reasons. Here, distinguished writers
address the issue of censorship in a
complex and fragile world where people with
widely different cultural habits and beliefs are
living in close proximity, where offence is easily
taken, and where words, images and behaviour
are coming under the closest scrutiny.
These books will surprise, clarify and provoke
in equal measure.

Index on Censorship is the only international
magazine promoting and protecting free
expression. A haven for the censored and
silenced, it has built an impressive track record
since it was founded 35 years ago, publishing
some of the finest writers, sharpest analysts and
foremost thinkers in the world. In this series
with Seagull Books, the focus will be on
questions of rights, liberties, tolerance,
silencing, censorship and dissent.

WHO DO YOU THINK YOU ARE?

the search for argentina's lost children

ANDREW GRAHAM-YOOLL

LONDON NEW YORK CALCUTTA

Seagull Books 2011

© Andrew Graham-Yooll 2010

ISBN-13   978 1 9064 9 777 4

British Library Cataloguing-in-Publication Data
A catalogue record for this book is available
from the British Library

Typeset and designed by Seagull Books, Calcutta, India
Printed at Graphic Prints, Calcutta

CONTENTS

ACKNOWLEDGEMENTS

Estela Barnes de Carlotto, President of Grandmothers of Plaza de Mayo, Buenos Aires, for assistance with background and legislation.

Rosa Roisinblit, Vice President of Grandmothers of Plaza de Mayo, for her persistent work and ready support.

Analía Lanza, of the Comisión Nacional por el Derecho a la Identidad (CoNaDI), Buenos Aires, for bibliography and background.

Marta Betoldi, Bruno Luciani and Patricia Zangaro, playwrights, for permission to translate into English and publish their plays.

Benjamín Prado, for his articles in the newspaper *El País*, Madrid.

Dr Alan Iud, lawyer, at the legal department of the Grandmothers of Plaza de Mayo.

Cecilia Vicuña, for permission to quote from her Introduction to the *Oxford Book of Latin American Poetry* (2009).

Janet Henfrey and Stella Maris Poncé, who arranged the staging in 2003 of three plays in translation at the Arcola theatre, London. Janet Henfrey was then head of the International Committee for Artists' Freedom (ICAF), a section of Equity, the actors' union.

Ursula Owen, editor, for lasting support at *Index on Censorship*.

Judith Vidal-Hall, editor and dear colleague, for 30 years of friendship and work together.

Poster of the 'disappeared' created by the Mothers of Plaza de Mayo.
Photograph: Pepe Robles.

A QUESTION OF IDENTITY

Who do you think you are? The question may seem rude, but it cannot be dismissed simply as impertinence. The second half of the twentieth century, from the Second World War on, witnessed the greatest movement of human beings ever. Voluntary or not, displacement often causes assimilation as somebody else. Migration, too, sometimes causes loss of environment and of identity.

Who do you think you are? Millions of people are not sure. Expatriation, exile, sickness, confinement, bereavement and authoritarian rule have all caused the transformation of individuals into non-persons—a concept illustrated in the work of the French anthropologist Marc Augé, who, in the 1990s, devised the label 'non-places' for shopping malls, because they are alien to all identity, rationality and history. By way of a brief historical survey covering individual and social identity in history, this essay will arrive at a short narrative on the consequences of the policies of the military government of Argentina in the 1970s when a plan was devised to 'disappear' the enemy, to make them 'non-existent'.

Who do you think you are? Socially in-correct, perhaps, but is it? When a conversation is about identity, it produces immediate certainties. We know by whom we were be-gotten, where we were born. Press the matter

further—as was tried in conversation with
students for this exercise—and invariably
some doubt sets in. If this happens when the
delving is at an individual level and with few
participants, doubt grows as one probes
deeper into ancestry and community life.
Sometimes, nostalgia takes the place of reality and the longing for something remote
becomes an exercise distorted by sentiment.
Memory becomes shadowy, a cloudy reflec-
tion of the past. Recollection loses its power
to hold real images, and certain aspects of
identity are thrown into doubt.

By the third time of asking, the question 'Who do you think you are?' becomes
vague. Identity is a moving, changing and
transforming element. We are not the same
people as begotten by our parents and their
parents, but we inherit traditions, customs,
and forms of belonging and of speech—
factors that build an identity from early
childhood. And it is from childhood that

authoritarian systems, political and religious, try to reshape pertinent facts, often by denying them.

Globalized society has been encouraged to accept that identity is an asset that takes second place to material comfort and middle-class success, and can only be invoked, waved or even brandished by people in authority or powerful figures in the arts and politics. By accepting these terms of existence, the loss of identity also becomes acceptable and could lead to the loss of social memory.[1]

Does the social memory of communities grow or fade with the passing years? The ageing individual will say that the clarity of recollection declines. However, the antidote to this is that time placates fear; changing circumstances in the law and government help draw out forgotten scenes. New generations want to know, and demand that their elders produce accounts of the hidden age.

In Argentina, the children of the 'disappeared' have become the most militant seekers of memory. They call it their 'search for identity'. For some, the recovery of their identity at birth may never happen. Strangely, the psychological effect of this on a whole society has been, initially, one of apprehension, in no way vengeful, often with attempted indifference. People seem to accept that Argentina will have to go through the long torment of remembering the past in every case that goes to trial for as long as there are 'repressors' of the 1970s still alive.

From such a broad view, it is possible to descend to historical, social and international circumstances and political events—some of them now taken for granted—or down to local tragedies that take place on a smaller scale, because the numbers involved and the territory covered is limited.

In the present exercise, the experience imposed on Argentina by the commanders

of a military dictatorship who held sway
over life and death comes in for scrutiny as
a by-product of the cold war. These chiefs
installed the concept of the 'disappeared' in
western languages. The word *desaparecidos*
had been in use for some time with various
applications, but it was a pusillanimous individual who had devoted his career to
climbing ranks—General Jorge Rafael
Videla, President of Argentina (March
1976–March 1981)—who endowed the sta-
tus of vanished human beings with mystery
and terror. At a meeting with foreign press
representatives in 1978 (still at the height
of the terror campaign, in the year of the
football World Cup) General Videla was
asked to explain the situation of the 'disappeared'. With a flip of both hands he ex-
plained, 'The disappeared do not exist,
they are not alive nor dead, they simply do
not exist.' ('*Los desaparecidos no existen, no
están ni vivos ni muertos, simplemente no existen.*') Lost as persons, they had vanished

and were no longer with us—they no longer had an identity.

However, before we can look at the nature and effect of the military campaign in Argentina, and the later publicity campaigns or counter-action of opponents after the dictatorship, it is useful to look through some recent history, and even further back, at events that inspired the South American generals.

In a twentieth-century catalogue of horror, it is inevitable that the Holocaust suffered by the Jewish people of Germany and Central Europe must top the list. The cruelty of state policy in the 12-year-long Nazi rule is without parallel. Many see the earlier genocide of the Armenians by the Turkish authorities during the First World War as the forerunner and closest parallel to the Holocaust. Indeed, the term 'genocide' was coined to describe the persecution of the Armenians that resulted in the loss of up to 1.5 million lives.

But a combination of ideology, national sentiment and some statistics places the greatest domestic slaughter in modern history in the Soviet Union, where Joseph Stalin's deadly purges continued almost up to his death in March 1953. Simon Sebag Montefiore quotes Nikita Khrushchev as telling Winston Churchill that the drive against the Kulaks took 10 million lives: 'They did not even specify the names but simply assigned quotas of deaths by the thousands.'[2] However, most recent research has considerably reduced this figure.[3]

The human cost of Mao Zedong's Great Leap Forward (1958–61) and, almost at the end of his life, the Cultural Revolution (1966–76), was set in millions so vast the numbers remain vague: 'between 50 and 70 million', anonymous, too many to list, forgotten. This loss of identity in numbers is perhaps most graphically illustrated by the stacks of bones of the victims of Pol Pot

(Saloth Sar, to give him his real identity) in Cambodia during the regime imposed in 'Democratic Kampuchea' (1975–79). The skulls and limb bones of many of the 200,000 executed, out of an estimated 1.5 million people 'disappeared', offer a landscape of horror. But they are just bones. The once-living people that functioned around those bones are lost; they were farm workers, teachers, technicians, medics and engineers—but we will never know who they were. Whoever those bones were as people and whatever they did has been, and shall be, omitted by history.

And we will probably never know—and this emphasizes the loss of identity—the extent of the killings under Kim Il Sung who took over in North Korea after the country was split into two in 1953.

These events are landmarks of horror in the twentieth century. And there are, of course, more. Almost at the tail end of the

century, when humanity was comforting itself with the advances achieved in the sci-
ences and other disciplines, when progress
of a material and technical kind moved
faster than at any other period since the be-
ginning of time, humanity found its way
back to the worst cruelty.

A case now entered in legal annals had
been in the making in Africa for years: the
genocide in Rwanda was brewing long before the slaughter broke out. The civil war
between Hutus and Tutsis that had been
festering since 1990 culminated in an orgy
of slaughter that saw at least 800,000 Tutsis
and moderate Hutus killed in little more
than three months. Only a few years
earlier, in the mid-1980s, the World Bank
had described Rwanda as a model of
development.[4]

Yet perhaps because the stage was Central Europe, at a time when Western Europe
was celebrating a triumphant end to the

cold war with the fall of the Berlin Wall in November 1989, the break up of the Soviet Union two years later and the prospect of a reunited Europe after almost 50 years of division, the war in the Balkans that broke out in 1991 hit the West and its network of smug and calculating political leaders with far greater shock and fury than events in Rwanda.

Slovenia was the first to declare independence from united Yugoslavia and got away relatively lightly. Croatia was next but the story was very different. Between August and November 1991, the Yugoslav Army—largely manned by Serbs—laid siege to the town of Vukovar in a by-now rapidly crumbling Yugoslavia. The destruction of Vukovar was accompanied by the decision to rob the people not just of their lives and properties—quite normal in a state of war—but also of their past by destroying records of their history and identity. The aim of wiping out a people and all that could identify them became known as 'ethnic cleansing'. The label, horrifying in itself, is, however, too gentle a description for a process of murder, displacement and rape that rained on the city in the course of the 87-day siege.

But what happened in the officially protected UN 'safe' area of Srebrenica in Bosnia and Herzegovina some four years later puts Vukovar in the shade. In July 1995, in the presence of UN troops, 8,000 Bosnian men and boys were massacred and buried in mass graves, and 25,000–30,000 made refugees in a process of ethnic cleansing, all carried out by units of the Army of the Republika Srpska (Vojsha Republic Srpshe). It was the biggest mass murder in Europe since the Second World War and officially labelled genocide by the International Criminal Tribunal for the former Yugoslavia (ICTY) in The Hague in 2004.

In all these cases—Armenia, the Soviet Union, Germany, Serbia, Rwanda and China—the slaughter was planned by educated men and women who went about destroying large numbers of their fellow nationals in carefully devised strategies. The ultimate aim in each of these policies of annihilation was the removal of a native characteristic. And whatever forms the policies took, and however sophisticated the citizens of the metropolis were, their intention was devastation: the obliteration of peoples, cultures, religious practices, forms of commerce; in short, anything that identified the community in question and made them different or 'other'.

Each of the events above had their origin in some of the important moments of history, in wars of conquest and their consequences. But it was the Spanish conquest of the Americas that set a precedent for the world: the justification was not simply the spread of the Christian gospel among the unknown natives of a large section of the world, but the creation of a new identity for the commercial benefit of a remote court. This development is concisely covered by Cecilia Vicuña in her essay, 'An Introduction to Mestizo Poetics' (2009):

> To understand the complex forces at play we must return to the moment when the European and indigenous worldviews first collided. This was a clash so powerful that it destroyed Amerindian cultures, giving birth to modernity. The conquest of America engendered Europe's cultural and economic development. The Argentine philosopher Enrique Dussel calls this the 'myth of modernity', 'a particular myth of sacrificial violence' that rationalizes European 'superiority' and its right to conquer, while occluding the rights of the 'other'. In [Dussel's] view, its emergence began a process of 'concealment or misrecognition of the non-European' that subsumed the contribution of the

peoples of Asia, Africa and the Americas to world culture.[5] As a result, the destruction of native cultures was never seen as a loss, only a necessary by-product of progress—a view that persists today [. . .]

In 1492, the Europeans did not arrive at a wilderness but to a densely populated land with advanced civilizations and, in the case of Mesoamerica, a literary tradition two thousand years older than that of Europe. Within a few decades it was destroyed.[6]

Three and a half centuries later, in Spain, the 'process of concealment or misrecognition' was extended to include its own nationals in the course of the Spanish Civil War (1936–39). The ideological distortions and the human consequences lingered, shrouded in silence, for decades up to the present day. The construct eventually became the advance model for that imposed in Argentina.

FABRICATING THE PAST

[Spain's] coup leaders of 1936 not only sought to exterminate their rivals, as shown in the more than 150,000 people buried in common graves which the Supreme Court has not allowed lower courts to open [. . .] but also to eradicate the ideology of their opponents. The plan was to seize the children of Republicans and through them spread the nationalist doctrine of hatred against the ideas of their families. In that moral swamp, some, such as a military officer and psychiatrist, Antonio Vallejo Nájera, in his absurd books developed the theory that Marxism is a mental illness—and catchy at that—so the chaff had to be parted from the wheat as stated by the regime's heralds. So, when the homes of the Social Rescue (Auxilio Social), the charitable organization founded by Mercedes Sanz Bachiller, widow of Falangist leader Onésimo Redondo, were filled with orphans and sons of prisoners and

the prisons housed hundreds of women
who were pregnant or with small children in their charge, the child thieves
had a large stock from where to select
their booty. Soon after the end of the war
[General Francisco] Franco passed two
laws to give this process a sense of legal-
ity. One of these, transferred control of
all children in the Social Rescue service
to the State, which was thereby free to
change their names and hand them to
whom the government wished. Babies
were seized shortly after birth at the
Prison for Nursing Mothers in Madrid
and their mothers were executed. Many
children were abducted from concentra-
tion camps beyond Spain's borders [. . .]
According to figures compiled by historian Ricard Vinyes, of 32,037 children
taken out of Spain by their parents,
20,266 were repatriated [. . .]

How many people in this country
are not who they think they are? According to figures in the courts, the total

number of children of prison inmates in 1955 was 31,000, as Franco reported directly to the central office of Our Lady of Mercy for the Redemption of Prison Sentences. Some victims remember being given for adoption and returned more than once, therefore becoming the owners of up to four surnames. One internal document showed that matters were running out of control because some people took children not to raise them as their own but to make them work on the land or in houses as slave labour.[7]

The preceding paragraphs are from an article published in the newspaper *El País* by the Spanish journalist Benjamín Prado. He had taken an interest in the subject of the missing children through adults whom he had found were not who they said they were. These encounters led to a novel, *Mala gente que camina* (Bad People who Walk, 2006), the title taken from a poem by Antonio Machado.[8] The story is a crime

novel without a body and describes the lives
of two women and the child of one of them
who live in the secret knowledge that they
are not who their documents say they are.
The novel was in some ways ahead of its
time for a wider audience because, when
published in 2006, Prado was surprised at
the number of people convinced that his
writing was a complete fabrication.[9]

Fiction has helped on many fronts, not
so much in determining identities but in
creating awareness of their absence. Perhaps the heaviest volume of fiction on
record, and especially in the US, must be
that associated with tracking down the ancestry and identity of families uprooted
from Africa and shipped in chains in one of
the most disgusting trades ever plotted and
developed by man.[10] Quite apart from the
many extensive, detailed and comprehen-
sively researched historical studies, it has
been fiction that has captured the public

imagination: that there was something es-
sentially wrong with mankind if we readily
put a store-price on each others' heads
which allowed for complete power over life
and death of the individual purchased. The
impact was achieved without doubt by
American author Alex Haley, whose novel
Roots: the Saga of an American Family (1976),
made into a successful television miniseries
in 1977, captured the sympathy and imagination of the public around the world.[11]
The story purported to be the life of the author's great-grandfather, captured by slave-
traders and emancipated in 1865, with a
record of his background and descendants.

This theme has been further developed
by the later writings of Nobel Prizewinner
Toni Morrison,[12] notably in her novel
Beloved (1987), and even, dare one say,
in the earlier work of American novelist
and travel writer Erskine Caldwell, among
others.[13]

In South America—even though Colombia was one of the major markets for African slaves—the outlook for fiction has not thrived, except in Brazil, which has taken the subject more in its stride. There are two outstanding books. One is by Ana Miranda, *Bay of All Saints and Every Conceivable Sin* (1992),[14] a first novel which gives Africans a strong role in the defence of the Portuguese colony against the Dutch invasion from 1624. The other is by now used as a source of historical reference, Antônio Olinto's *The Water House*.[15] It is the story of a group of emancipated slaves who decide to return to their own country, the British colony of Nigeria, to recover their homes and identities. By the time of their return, at the end of the nineteenth century, they were Portuguese-speaking Roman Catholics and as such had lost touch with their original selves. The returnees, on whom the novel is based, were responsible for the construction of the Catholic cathedral in Lagos and, according to historians, for reintroducing the Yoruba language that had almost been lost during colonization.

But fiction produces strange effects on the public and, in many ways, on the history that follows. One example is the US television series *Holocaust* (1978), directed by Marvin Chomsky, which, when shown in West Germany, sparked a reaction of guilt, awareness and self-scrutiny about the extent of the Nazi horrors. No earlier documentation had produced such a reaction. Such widespread sentiment had not even been sparked by the de-Nazification campaign after the Second World War, perhaps because—as the British poet Stephen Spender, then working with the UK occupation forces explains—the policy aimed to counter the Nazi effect on the population without identifying the criminal architects, for fear of perpetuating their presence.

Fiction has not been so generous with the history of the Gypsies, in part due, perhaps, to their own levels of illiteracy and poor education, as described in Isabel Fonseca's intrepid report of the Roma in Central Europe.[16] In the acknowledgements in her book Fonseca thanks Turkish-born British novelist Musa Moris Farhi for his help and research. Farhi produced a substantial novel in English on the Roma in which the opening anecdote is the ultimate acknowledgement of an identity crisis. The story told by the Gypsy chroniclers he met in Macedonia and elsewhere in pre-war Yugoslavia was that the original Book of the Roma was written on cabbage leaves, which were eaten by one of their donkeys.[17] Given the persecution suffered by the Roma under Hitler in Germany and the Ustasha (Nazi collaborators in Croatia, Hungary and other countries occupied by the Nazis) it would be natural to expect them to be better represented in fiction. The reality within Europe is even more sordid. The persecution of Travellers' children—loosely associated with Gypsies even if not of the same stock—to suppress their identity, thrived through much of the twentieth century in Switzerland:

> In its effort to erase the nomadic way of life of its Gypsy population, Switzerland kidnapped almost 600 Yenitsche children from their parents over a 50-year period, from 1926 until 1973. Pro Juventute, a foundation created in 1912 with the stated goal of working for the good of children, young people and their families, placed such children with host families and in orphanages, psychiatric hospitals and even penal institutions. That was how Swiss society tried to get rid of Travellers. 'Constant travelling, alcoholism, immorality and an indescribable indigence are the common lot of these families,' wrote Alfred Siegfried

(1890–1972), director of the Mutual Aid Society for the Children of the Roads, set up in 1926, in the Swiss newspaper of record, the *Neue Zürcher Zeitung* (founded in 1780). He urged that despite the lack of money, despite the fear of hereditary taint, attempts be made at least to save the children. The Yenitsche, who made up the majority of Swiss Travellers, were seen as criminals—lazy, tainted and incapable of bringing up their own children. Siegfried took children from their parents because he believed that constant travelling had its roots in family relationships. 'Those who wish to truly fight this constant wandering must try to break the ties that bind Travellers: he must, however hard it may seem, tear apart families. There are no other solutions,' he wrote in 1943 [. . .] Parents who opposed the abduction of their children were themselves put under legal guardianship and the Society systematically erased all traces of

such proceedings, so that parents could
not find where their children had been
placed. In cases where children were
badly treated by host families or in insti-
tutions, they were given no protection by
Pro Juventute.[18]

The Roma in Europe continues to be the
most persecuted group throughout the Eu-
ropean Union. Despite legislation against
racism and discrimination, the community
has received virtually no legal redress and is
the victim of hate campaigns and discrimination in the media.

As suggested earlier, the Argentine experience in numbers hardly compares with
the 'bigger' tragedies of the twentieth century, though one might ask if numbers
alone constitute a significant measure of
evil. Even if the uncertain figure of 30,000
'disappeared' in the 1970s is taken as
valid—and it is an awkward and even em-
barrassing custom to use round numbers
to impress the extent of disasters because

generalization devalues the importance of the individual—the number of casualties in Argentina is small when taken in a historical context. The make-up of the figure of the 'disappeared' has been queried by the parent of one of the youths murdered by the military.[19] However, there are certain factors that make Argentina unique:

1. If measured in terms of literacy levels and development, what took place in the 1970s in the River Plate territories happened in one of the most advanced societies in South America.

2. The extent of 'repression' was arguably unnecessary by the time it was unleashed, because the guerrilla organizations had been largely defeated.

3. The trial of the leaders of the military regime was held by a democratically elected constitutional government under President Raúl Ricardo Alfonsín (1983–89), a weak

administration in contrast with the lingering might of the armed forces, and the proceedings have become examples of due process in international law.

4. The efforts made by authorities, and mainly by the organizations of relatives of the 'disappeared', to identify human remains in unmarked graves and to recover the children of captives executed by the dictatorship have become an example for human rights groups everywhere. South African lawyers and politicians took the Argentine model and improved it in the search for truth about Apartheid.

5. The use of forensic anthropology and DNA resources in linking parents of the dead with surviving grandchildren, for example, was pioneered in Buenos Aires and has become a vital development in determining identities.

andrew graham-yooll

ARGENTINA: A SUITABLE CASE FOR TREATMENT

But why Argentina, when it is obvious that
despite the horror of the dictatorship in the
1970s the case is small in comparison with
most contemporary horrors?

The easiest answer is that what has
been done since the fall of the military,
known as 'the last dictatorship', is worthy of
interest worldwide. The effort has been
aimed at defeating indifference in a society
while recovering individual and social identities. Though the full story of the policies
and the victims of the military may never be
known, the experience may help to set pat-
terns of awareness and responsibility for the
widest possible audience.

Former President and now former
General Videla took office soon after his
colleagues, the heads of the army, air force
and navy, seized power on 24 March 1976.
The coup did not involve military might; it
was the overthrow of an elected but weak

and corrupt government led by María Estela Martínez Cartas de Perón, widow of
General Juan Domingo Perón, who had
died on 1 July 1974, nine months into his
third term as president (his previous two
terms ran from 1946 to 1955).

Although Argentina had lived through
eight military regimes between September
1930 and March 1976, the last coup came
with a difference: it had a real armed
enemy. There were two active urban guerrilla organizations: one a nationalist group
known as Montoneros—a name with its origins in the nineteenth-century provincial
private armies formed by land barons—that
started as followers of Perón; and the Marx-
ist-Leninist People's Revolutionary Army
(Ejécito Revolucionario del Pueblo or ERP),
which also had a rural branch operating in
northern Argentina. They were daring, not
strong, and, by the time of the March 1976
coup, many of their leaders were dead, in
prison or had fled abroad. However, the

remaining guerrillas were still able to stage spectacular strikes.

A further difference between this coup and previous ones was that in the 1970s, with the cold war in full force, Argentina's armed forces were convinced—as were other dictators in South America—that their country was the target of a world conspiracy to install Cuban-style systems in the region. Washington encouraged that assumption, developed at all war colleges. What the theory ignored was that the youth of several countries (Brazil, Uruguay, Argentina and others) had been barred from political participation for more than a generation. The military plan in Argentina was to destroy their enemy and wipe out its ideology by 'first going for the activists, then for the sympathizers and finally for the indifferent'.[20] The aim was to capture the enemy alive, apply unlimited torture to secure information, execute the captive and 'disappear' the body. Thus the military contributed new meaning to the Spanish word, *desaparecido*. Bodies were disposed of in unmarked mass graves or thrown from planes into the South Atlantic.[21]

As stated earlier, General Videla is recorded as saying that the 'disappeared' did not exist, they simply were 'not here any more'. He is seen waving his arms to illustrate the vanishing act. Military policy represented the censorship of memory, an attempt to deny the existence of its rivals. Such a project for unchallenged rule required a binding pact of secrecy which would eventually and inevitably be broken by some participants, but which had been largely upheld by the senior officers responsible, a discourse of terror,[22] and the support of the establishment, including the country's established religion.[23] When journalists demanded information at fairly high levels of government, the pact of secrecy was used to avoid the kind of unfavourable publicity suffered by the regime of General Augusto Pinochet in Chile following the September 1973 coup.[24]

The 'disappearing'—now a verb—of enemies was a para-official policy before the coup of March 1976, because a para-military organization had been in operation with full government support—finance, arms and legal cover—even during the final brief nine-month administration of Perón from October 1973 to June 1974. It was known as the Triple A (Argentine Anticommunist Alliance) and had its headquarters in the basement of the Social Welfare Ministry, led by a sinister character and former secretary to Perón, José López Rega, known as El Brujo (The Warlock). The members of this group had a method of terror which included riddling their victims' bodies with bullets (up to 70 shots—as the ammunition supply was free), burning the bodies with the limbs tied with wire and burying the dead in unmarked graves. The targets were identified as 'left-wing' opponents, guerrillas, trade unionists, politicians, university students and lecturers. The military coup built on this background.

While it showed no qualms in 'disappearing' victims—Chilean and Uruguayan refugees who sought asylum in Argentina following the coups in their countries were also targets—it is still open to debate whether the military came to government in Buenos Aires with the aim of eliminating the children of their captives.

There are two views. The most strongly held one—that the military planned forced adoption under new identities of the children of captured militants—comes from the 'Grandmothers of Plaza de Mayo', a group set up in 1977 by women from the 'Mothers of Plaza de Mayo' to find the babies born in captivity to mothers who were later murdered. Another view, though not completely contrary, is that of Sara Méndez, an Uruguayan activist who had sought refuge in Buenos Aires after the coup in Montevideo in June 1973. Méndez was captured in Buenos Aires by Uruguayan security and intelligence agents, operating with official permission in Argentina as part of an inter-government agreement, in July 1976. Her 20-day-old baby was also abducted. However, she was lucky and recovered her child when both mother and baby were secretly transferred from Argentina to detention in Uruguay, where the captives had to sign testimonies that they had been arrested in their own country and had never been in Argentina.

In an essay on her own experience, Méndez says:

> I believe, and this is personal, that in the early stages of repression there was no plan to appropriate (abduct, rob, adopt) children as part of the 'systematic plan'

of the military [. . .] The change of plan
is a result of those early stages because
when a person is detained or abducted,
(and will later 'disappear' and, hence, all
traces of them had to be removed) only
then was it decided that children had to
suffer the consequences. It was difficult,
in a raid different from normal police
procedure, to leave children with a
neighbour or a relative because that
amounted to advising third parties that a
raid was under way. Hence, the original
circumstances changed.[25]

In contrast, the Grandmothers of Plaza de
Mayo argue that there was a clearly established plan to wipe out a section of society
described simply as 'terrorist subversives'
and that included their children because
they could constitute a danger in the future.
This could only be countered by 'state terror'. The Grandmothers set out to find
the children carried by the young women
and born in captivity then given away for

adoption. A list was compiled of nearly 500 children and youth, most of whose whereabouts were unknown. Some were dead (such as the 14-year-old girl who was considered a security threat) and most are yet to be found. But 99 individuals have been identified. Again, the numbers are small in a global context, but the search process has produced guidelines of international importance.

Argentina's military was forced to leave the government in December 1983 largely as a result of defeat in the Falklands/Malvinas war with UK in 1982. In 1985, the members of the military *juntas* (heads of the three armed services) who had held government during the seven years of dictatorship were tried and found guilty of crimes against humanity.[26] In 1990, they received a pardon; unlike an amnesty, which wipes the record, a pardon does not eliminate the crime, and this pardon had a clause that

excluded the abduction of children. Eight
years later, on 9 June 1998, former General
Videla was placed under house arrest on
charges of authorizing the abduction of babies born to mothers in captivity. In November 2009, he was cleared of some
charges. In August 2003, the National Con-
gress and the Supreme Court of Argentina
revoked the pardons of the 1990s as well as
the legislation passed in 1987 that had
cleared junior officers who had obeyed or-
ders under the doctrine of 'due obedience'.
Former senior officers who had escaped
prosecution—many of them old men now—
have gone back on trial for the crimes of
the 1970s. The government of the first
decade of the twenty-first century sought a
double impact with reversal of the pardons:
one, a political blow attractive to the left
wing and human rights groups; two, an attempt to show the world that serious efforts
were being made to recover full information and identities lost at that time.

CENSORING MEMORY

The problem with the recovery of full information and identity is that too much documentation has been lost. Some has been found, of course, but the bulk of records and files were destroyed by order of the last military president, General Reynaldo Bignone (sentenced to 25 years in prison in April 2010) before handing over power to civilian rule at the end of 1983. Thousands will never know the whereabouts of the bones of their next of kin, friends and children. Argentina has lost a considerable chunk of the story of a generation by the action of an archaic military establishment with its eyes set on 'ideological cleansing'. The missing children may never be found. This is not unique to Argentina, of course. Austrian-born British author Gitta Sereny remarked in one of her best-known books that Germany was still plagued by 'forgotten or misunderstood episodes, like the

Nazis' systematic abduction of Aryan-looking children from families in eastern Europe to give them to German parents'.[27]

In Argentina, too, the babies of blonde mothers were the most sought after prizes. As in Spain, the practice had deep roots. In a remarkable essay on the treatment of children in Argentina's history, child psychoanalyst and social analyst Jorge Volnovich, traces the path along which religious influence (since the struggle for independence started in 1810 and up to the most recent military rule) recommended that children be used to change the course of national life, sometimes by suppressing identities:

> The child, in 1810, filled the space of an adult in the social context, colonized in body and mind [. . .] As stated by an eminent priest and educator at the time, Francisco de Paula Castañeda, 'It is not enough that children learn the rudiments of Catholic religion which we have

the joy to profess, it is not enough that
they read, write and count, all this can be
acquired by day, the night must be used
in their instruction and learning [. . .]
Hence the Argentine child was born
under a patriarchal regime as a colo-
nized adult, clerical and military, a perfect slave.[28]

This model is what a part of modern
society wanted to see imposed. And as yet,
while there is legislation and government
action, there is no state policy framed in education or in society to reverse the system
installed in the mind for two centuries.
Volnovich emphasizes that the vigour with
which children are conditioned at an early
stage determines the strength of their sense
of identity and their ability to construct a
personal and social memory. Attention
span in children is one of the cornerstones
of education because it helps to build
memory which is a necessary part of identity; yet, society in the 1970s was intent on

developing a conditioned personality, a different identity, by altering memory through its censorship.

Now, the emphasis on the need to recover personal identities as a way to build a society is a politically attractive statement but not an easy process. The Volnovich quotation above might even support the argument that Argentina was born with an identity crisis: from Spanish colony to immigrant destination without a state policy of assimilation that recognized origins yet encouraged a new sense of belonging. From the mid-nineteenth century, Argentina, more than any other South American country, was built by immigrants. Most thought, not unreasonably, that identity was secondary to getting a job and making money. They had failed in their old countries, they had come to a new one where their names were wrongly spelt in public documents and nobody cared much about what they had left behind.

Again, resorting to fiction, the Yiddish
author and short-story writer Isaac Bashevis
Singer is a suitable reference here for his
warning to Jews against their loss of identity. Singer's story 'The Colony'[29] is based
on a visit he made to the Jewish community
in Argentina. While some of the author's
prejudices over the treatment he received—
largely a result of general ignorance of his
work and consequent indifference to his
visit—may have prompted some of the un-
flattering remarks, Singer did tell his inter-
viewer, Polish-born Argentinian Yiddish
writer Simha Sneh, that the spiritual void
and fading religious principles in the farm-
ing colonies, funded by Jewish-German
businessman Baron Moritz von Hirsch,
threatened the continuation of a Jewish
identity in Argentina.[30] 'Who would people
be, where would Jewishness be if they lost
awareness of their identity?' Singer asked,
according to Sneh. The fear was perhaps
misplaced: one aspect of the dictatorship's

officers was their fear of the strength of the Jewish community and it manifested in strong anti-Semitism.

SEARCHING FOR LIFE

The Mothers of Plaza de Mayo began the search for their 'disappeared' children in 1976, almost immediately after the coup. Tearful, clamouring parents were forced to queue in the square in front of Government House to await information they would never receive. The pleading parents were ordered by police to 'move on' and they circled the Plaza de Mayo. They still, in 2010, walk around the obelisk in Plaza de Mayo every Thursday at 3 p.m., continuing their campaign for information about the 'disappeared'. The Mothers became a high-profile organization which included the private University of the Mothers that opened in October 2000. The educational aim was to uphold not just the memory and the cause but also the somewhat Utopian aspirations of many of the young who died fighting. Human rights groups agree that the original report on the 'disappeared', *Nunca Más* (Never Again), is fundamental but its compilation of victims incomplete.[31]

A group of the Mothers eventually formed the Grandmothers of Plaza de Mayo to search for the grandchildren that some of the women were carrying when they were abducted and are known, or are strongly suspected, to have been born in captivity. In 1999, the Grandmothers got, in the words of US-Spanish historian Marysa Navarro, their first 'long-awaited story'.[32] Interestingly, the book in which this quote appears, by an expatriate Argentinian scientist, Rita Arditti, found no publisher in Argentina until a year after it was published in the US.

The surviving children of the 'disappeared' formed a militant group known as 'Hijos' (Offspring or Sons) to campaign for

the recovery of identity lost by abduction
and murder and also to identify the torturers and killers of the 1970s. At the end of
the twentieth century, this militant youth
group joined forces with the Grandmothers'
campaign 'to know who people really are'.
The campaign for the recovery of identity
gained further public exposure through the
theatre. A series of short plays were written,
inviting and inciting people with any doubt
about their identity at birth being different
from that of the present to seek help.[33] The
theatre series, which had a low-profile
opening in June 2000 on a university stage,
brought a substantial number of enquiries
but not many confirmations of stolen identities. However, the project gained international recognition and widespread publicity
which accelerated investigations and confir-
mation of fraudulent adoptions dating back
to 1976. By now, however, the 'babies' of
the 'disappeared' were in their mid-twenties
and, as young adults, found the courage to

come forward for blood tests and DNA
checks at the testing centre in the Durand
Hospital in Buenos Aires, where a bank of
genetic data was set up with the support
and guidance of US forensic medicine ex-
pert Clyde Snow.

In June 2000, the first play, *A propósito
de la duda* (*A Propos of Doubt*), had the feeling of street theatre taken to an indoor
stage. Written by playwright Patricia Zangaro, the 35-minute performance puts the
question from the stage, up front and 'in
your face'. The audience is asked, 'Who are
you?' and 'Do you know who you are? Are
you sure that the name you have been given
is really yours?' *A Propos of Doubt* broke new
ground in the contact with the public
through what was announced as 'Teatro X
la Identidad' (Theatre for Identity).[34]

The issue of memory and identity has
moved on to encompass the contemporary
traffic of children for prostitution, illegal

child labour and the alleged but not proven trade in children for organ transplants. The National Commission for the Right to Identity (Comisión Nacional por el Derecho a la Identidad, CoNaDI) was created in November 1992 as an office of the Secretariat for Human Rights, first under the Interior Ministry and later as part of the Justice Ministry. The office has to deal with the questions left unanswered by the military dictatorship as well as with the new issues precipitated by poverty, child labour, etc.[35]

In addition to the plays, the Grandmothers' campaign gained in strength and public recognition with the indication by President Néstor Kirchner, who took office on 25 May 2003, that he would make it national policy to get the tormentors of the 1970s into court. The problem with this initiative was that it did not include a provision to secure the fullest possible report on the events of that time in a bid to give history—at least that of Argentina—a clear explanation of what the country lived through during a recent decade. The political decision taken by President Kirchner omitted the next step: to make the past a matter of state.

Perhaps, the 'matter of state' can be developed in stages. In November 2009, three laws created a national genetics bank, a controversial ruling that allowed judges to demand DNA samples for identification purposes,[36] and granted human rights or other organizations the right to become plaintiff and initiate legal action in cases of suspected crimes against humanity.[37]

There are some legacies that the twentieth century bequeathed without explanation. It is not surprising that military regimes that seized power in what became one of the most highly literate countries in Latin America burned books,[38] destroyed universities and demolished cultural centres

in the name of combatting foreign ideolo-
gies and strange religions to erase a section
of society as an identity. Education was not
seen as a part of intellectual growth and
learning; it had to be part of an allegiance
to a male, military, chauvinistic fatherland
that would rise, pure and strong, above all
rivals. In that atmosphere it is not surprising either that society was encouraged to
dismiss the 'disappeared' simply because
they 'must have done something', with the
inevitable rider: 'Better not get involved.'

The Grandmothers have established for
themselves what might be considered a
strange target: telling people who they are
and showing the world that there are ways
of clarifying a wide variety of problems in-
herent in identity. The members of this
group are growing older, working against
time to incorporate more people into
awareness of the full scope of the problems
created by lack of identity. It is not an easy

task. What at first loomed as the impossible
pursuit of recovering the bones of people
long dead, discovering the identity of the
bones found and of the children the women
might have given birth to and, then,
educating society so that people are aware
that they have a right to know who they are,
still seems difficult. But people have begun
to accept these elements as reasonable, in
the hope that the 1970s do not happen
ever again.

DOCUMENTS: TWO PLAYS FROM TEATRO X LA
IDENTIDAD (THEATRE FOR IDENTITY)

From a series of short plays for the stage launched in June 2000, supported by the Grandmothers of Plaza de Mayo in Buenos Aires to promote awareness of the people who 'disappeared' during the dictatorship, their stolen babies and lost identities. These two plays, out of three published in English by *Index on Censorship*, are reprinted with the authors' permission.

A PROPOS OF DOUBT

(A propósito de la duda)

SCRIPT. Patricia Zangaro, based on statements collected by the Grandmothers of Plaza de Mayo.

DIRECTOR. Daniel Fanego.

First staged on Monday, 5 June 2000 at Rojas Theatre, University of Buenos Aires.

Translated from Spanish by Andrew Graham-Yooll, published in *Index on Censorship*, 1 (2001).

Actors assemble on darkened stage.

A spotlight shines on Boy bouncing a ball.

Sound of helicopter overhead. Boy leaves the ball and walks off.

Grandmother I picks up the ball, and shows it to two others who look on in distress.

Light on a couple of Appropriators—the name given to parents who have adopted a child of a 'disappeared' person. Seated on chairs, Man and Bald Youth who wears headphones connected to a Walkman. Woman stands behind Bald Youth, vigorously massaging his head.

GRANDMOTHER I (*wondering*). Is baldness hereditary?

GRANDMOTHER II (*thoughtful*). Baldness . . . is hereditary . . .

GRANDMOTHER III (*vehement*). Baldness is hereditary.

Male Appropriator laughs.

THREE GRANDMOTHERS. Baldness is hereditary!

MALE APPROPRIATOR. My son has the certainty that we are his parents. We have the documents, they are all in order. I do not need to go for any tests. To prove what? We are not going to be judged here. We are condemned in advance. Appropriators, torturers, repressors. That's what they say we are. I ask you if you see any sign of torture in the boy? All I know is that I have worked all my life as a policeman. I told the boy never to say that his father was a policeman. That is not lying. It is omission. Nobody lies in this house. Today, in Argentina, those of us who fought for our country are criminals. I think that I, and many more, deserve a monument instead of persecution. But putting aside the monument bit, they should leave us in peace at least. Not me, a soldier struggling against ignominy, but these poor innocents. They suffer the most. The family is being destroyed. Unfortunately,

human rights belong to the Left. We are
not human. We have no rights.

GRANDMOTHER I. For as long as there is
a single person with their identity
stolen . . .

WOMAN APPROPRIATOR (*interrupting*). They
want to take him from me! They talk
about identity. And what about all the
years he has lived with me? Eh? Is he
going to be born again? If there is anybody who is innocent in this situation, it
is my son. And now they want to con-
demn him to exile. I am and always will
be the mother. I brought up a healthy
son. I have to care for the physical and
mental health of my son. I am not
going to allow them to sicken him with
hatred and resentment. Do you want
me to read the letter he wrote to me
when he was 10 years old?

MALE APPROPRIATOR (*uncomfortable, whispers
in her ear*). Not now. This isn't the right
time.

WOMAN APPROPRIATOR (*who has already un-folded a piece of paper and put on her read-ing glasses*).

'Mother most courageous,
'Who cares for me with love,
'You are the most beautiful rose
'Who spares me from pain.
'When at night I wake
'From my sad nightmares
'You cure my wounds
'With your love sincere.
'Do not walk out of my life,
'Mother dear, I love you!'

THREE GRANDMOTHERS. For as long as there is a single person with their identity stolen and forged, the identity of all is in doubt.

Woman Appropriator embraces Bald Youth.

BALD YOUTH. I was lucky. I have a family, a career, a car. I feel like Number One. I am great with women. Just like my dad. He says that when he was in the force

he shagged them all. The only thing
that screws me is my baldness. My dad,
the old dog, has hair coming out of his
ears. But when he was young he was
bald, just like me . . .
(*He stops, confused*)
I was lucky. When I get my degree my
dad promised to give me a hair im-
plant. He doesn't like baldies. He says
they look like faggots, that he feels like
grabbing them and busting their balls.
My mother, just in case, spends her
time massaging my head. Better hairy
than with busted balls, like my dad . . .
(*He stops, confused*)
I was lucky. When my hair grows I'll be
just like my dad. I am going to fuck
everything. I am going to run right
over the world. I am going to grab all the
baldies and bust their balls. I don't like
baldies. They are just like my dad . . .

*Bald Youth stops. He is concerned about the
accusing look of Woman Appropriator.*

YOUNG WOMAN I (*approaches him and whis-pers*). It is not the same to belong to a place as to look as if you do.

(*Bald Youth looks at her.*)

My mother said: 'Give me the fork.' It was a film of a family birthday. She was there for a second, and said: 'Give me the fork.' My mother was eight months pregnant when they took her. I was born in Pozo de Banfield.[39] A police-woman appropriated me. I must have rewound the film 20 times. My mother, all the time, said: 'Give me the fork. Give me the fork.' It is the only image I have of her alive. I never wanted to see the policewoman again, not even to swear at her. If somebody lies to you about something so basic, which is who you are, where you come from . . . How can you not doubt every word she says? Deep down one knows. It is not the same to belong to a place as to look as if you do. I love to go on Sundays to my grandparents' to eat pasta. My uncles go there, so do my cousins. Every time I say, 'Give me the fork,' I laugh. I don't know, it is as if I feel that my mother is there. Not her absence, her presence.

Sound of the helicopter returns. Young Woman runs off. Three Grandmothers approach Appropriators, who retreat, indignant.

GRANDMOTHER I. My daughter was kidnapped when she was six months pregnant. I know she had a boy. I am looking for him.

GRANDMOTHER II. My three children disappeared. Graciela, the youngest, was about to give birth. I have no information on any of them.

GRANDMOTHER III. My daughter-in-law was pregnant when she was abducted with my son Ignacio. I was told that a girl was born at the Military Hospital. I am still looking for her.

Man in the stalls starts to shout.

MAN. Just a minute! I cannot keep quiet. I have something to say. When the Coup happened I had just finished my Border Guard training. We were confined to barracks and then I was transferred to Mobile Unit I at Campo de Mayo,[40] which was a detachment trained to fight guerrillas. I was assigned to several groups, in the city and outside the capital. I was in the Olimpo Brigade.[41] My job was to drive the prisoners. I transported them from one place to another, or to the Metropolitan Airport, or to Ezeiza Airport. I drove a truck sto—
(*He looks around*)
—stolen from the Bruckman Brothers family, just like all the unit's vehicles. The prisoners were heavily sedated, and unconscious, they were delirious sometimes. On the last journey I had to take a woman who was about to give

63

birth. I was never told what was going
to happen to the prisoners, but one
could imagine it. I saw several pregnant
women at Olimpo. I took one captured
woman to the Military Hospital, and
that was where an intelligence officer
took charge of the child. It was a way of
protecting them, so that they would not
grow up in a subversive atmosphere.
The mother was dead. She was taken
back to the base, and from there to
Puente Doce, where the bodies were
cremated in large vats. Tyres were
thrown in, and then petrol, then the
body was thrown in, and then more
tyres. I feel no weight on my conscience
because I never killed anybody. I only
transported the prisoners.

*A group of youth assembles and starts a sur-
prise and noisy* escrache *demonstration to
identify and draw attention to Man. They
shout 'Murderer! Assassin!'*

Bald Youth begins to walk off, but Boy intercepts him.

BOY. I was torn from my parents' arms. My grandmother is still searching for me.

CHORUS OF YOUTH (*to the sound of the drums beating in the* escrache).[42] And you, do you know who you are?

YOUNG WOMAN II (*going to face Bald Youth*). My brother has just had his 20th birthday. I am still looking for him. I had imagined him as a little nuisance with whom I would some day be able to play. It is hard to believe that we will never have what we did not share, what we did not say to each other.

GRANDMOTHER I. It is not just the voice of the blood calling.

GRANDMOTHER II. It is the call of the soul.

GRANDMOTHER III. It is the voice of my daughter who demands that I find my grandchildren.

CHORUS OF YOUTH. And you, do you know
who you are?

YOUNG MAN I (*going to Bald Youth*). I only
recently learned the story of my life.
The memories were cloudy because I
was five years old the day they took my
parents, my uncles and my grandparents. They left my brother and me in
the park holding our toys. The memories are a blur, but we have memories.

CHORUS OF YOUTH. And you, do you know
who you are?

BOY. The most important thing is to know
who you are. Everybody has to know
who they are, if not they are nobody, or
think they are someone else.

YOUNG WOMAN IV. I wonder how long the
appropriators think they can go on
cheating us?

YOUNG MAN II (*to Bald Youth*). I want to
know if I have a brother. I dream of

him, a little brother who is 22 years old.
I need him because he is a part of who I
am. What hurts is not just the doubt but
the lies.

GRANDMOTHER I. I am 70 years old, and I
have been searching for 20. The love
for our missing kin is what drives us.
Not knowing where one has come from
is like floating in the air, without any
roots.

CHORUS OF YOUTH. And you, do you know
who you are?

BOY. My granny is looking for me. Help
her to find me.

*Bald Youth begins to leave, looking very
disturbed.*

YOUNG MAN III (*calling after Bald Youth*).
Baldy! They say I have the same way of
crossing my arms. Like this. As if I was
cradling a child. My father disappeared
when I was four years old. My family

said that he had gone to Tierra del
Fuego. But I do not look like him.
That's what they say. But I think I have
something of his at the edge of my
mouth. Like this, like a smile. Can you
imagine what it means to have your
own family lying to you? Of course, you
can't see these things in photographs:
I would like to know how he held his
cigarette, how he went for a crap, or if
he liked eating sardines. Even if they lie
to you, deep down you know. Some
mornings when I wake up I don't know
why I have such a strong desire to eat
sardines.

Frozen. That's how my father looks.
Frozen in a photograph as a kid. But he
was a living person, wasn't he? He may
have had a nervous tic in his mouth,
like a smile. Maybe he ate sardines, like
I do. It would be wonderful if the photo
suddenly started moving. If it started to

talk, or laugh, or swear, or just say a lot of stupid things. He might cross his arms, as if he was cradling a child, like this, just like me. And you, who are you?

CHORUS OF YOUTH. And you, do you know who you are?

GRANDMOTHER II. In 20 years none of us will be alive, but the search will go on for all those who have doubts about being the children of a lost generation.

GRANDMOTHER I. Every person we find is as if we have found our own grandchild.

YOUNG WOMAN IV (*walking towards Bald Youth; she is heavily pregnant*). Torture during pregnancy, parturition in captivity, separation from the mother shortly after birth . . . That is written in some part of the soul. I hope that some day, now, or in 40 years, my brother will start searching.

CHORUS OF YOUTH. And you, do you know
who you are?

Drums and Chorus louder and louder.

Blackout.

IN LABOUR

(*Contracciones*)

SCRIPT. Marta Betoldi.

DIRECTOR. Leonor Manso.

First staged on Tuesday, 8 October 2002 at the Sala Del Nudo Theatre, Buenos Aires.

Translated from Spanish by Andrew Graham-Yooll, published in *Index on Censorship*, 1 (2003).

Stage is in darkness. Stage left: a light shines on Andrea, a woman aged 42. She looks younger. Her clothes are brightly coloured. She sits at a desk writing a letter which she reads aloud.

ANDREA. Hello son, or daughter. I've just had the tests which explain my morning sickness. It's my birthday today and I want to thank you for this present. I'm a little shocked, but happy. Dad knows nothing yet. I thought you should be the first to learn of your existence. I'll put the tests here.

The written word, I think, suits me better to speak my feelings. I am usually quiet and shy, you will soon see, but this moment is so big I think I must be as talkative as possible. Oh, we've had your name for ages. Juan if you're a boy, Laura if you are lucky enough to be the stronger sex. And as I know about these things . . . I am sure you are Laura.

*A light goes up stage right to show Laura, a
woman aged 23, seated at a desk writing a
letter. When action moves to Laura, Andrea
continues to write in silence.*

LAURA. Today I was told what a mother's
intuition had heard from the heart.
The tests showed you're a real . . . girl.
Dad was a little crestfallen. He's quite
a macho, even if he denies it. I am
delighted.

I didn't start writing earlier without
knowing all was well, and you are! I am
a manic letter-writer, to my mother's
regret. She even threw out the letters I
wrote as a teenager to an imaginary
boyfriend. This is a secret diary that
belongs to you and me. The others will
only see the scans and the photos.

ANDREA. Mum says that letter-writing is a
family habit I've got from Granny
Antonia. The story goes that when
she stopped being illiterate she wrote

letters to the whole village. I hope I pass down the best of us. Dad is besotted: he has already bought six pairs of booties.

I think you are going to be a Taurus, according to my astrologer aunt. The sun will give you beauty, the arts and a strong character, pigheaded even. To me you will be perfect, whatever your date of birth.

LAURA. You will be born in October, like me, unless you decide otherwise. I saw you on the screen today, so clearly! You were sucking a finger on your right hand and looked happy, and you moved all the time like an astronaut as if you knew you were on film. I think you look like me. I think, because Mum doesn't have any pictures of me as a baby. The family photo albums were lost in one of our many moves. In my first 10 years, Dad's work had us

moving all over the country. I would
have liked to have at least one photo to
compare us. I'll make copies of everything, including the scans, and keep
them in a safe place.

ANDREA. I will stick this first photo of you
inside me and I hope you like it. I feel a
bit fat, but I've never felt so lovely and
radiant.

LAURA. It's time we decided a name. I
don't want to go on calling you Daughter. Even if it sounds big it is not
enough. It's a difficult choice, difficult
for me. A name is like a face. A person
in itself, a name speaks of who you are.
I've almost decided on María, which
your Dad likes and . . .

ANDREA. Laura. Don't let anybody call you
Laurita, Lala, Luli, or anything like
that. I've always disliked nicknames.
You are Laura.

LAURA. Laura? Not Martina. Why did I write Laura? Laura? It doesn't sound right. It sounds better with my surname, Laura González.

ANDREA. Laura Olivares. It's strong, has personality. 'Hello, Miss Laura Olivares. How are you today?'

LAURA. I am feeling fine, though I still vomit. They say that stops after three months.

ANDREA. I am in the fourth month and I still have to open the window in the bus, and hang onto trees. The vomiting doesn't stop. The doctor says that's normal, just nerves. I have trouble studying, I feel sleepy all the time. But I must get into Philosophy. Your dad is in his Psychology finals. I don't see him much now that he works at the Students' Union. He left me his photo. Nice Freud we have, eh? He has style. I love him so much, and he loves me. I feel so full today. I am happy.

LAURA. Sometimes I feel strange. I can't stop crying. There is a pressure in the middle of my chest, concentrated anxiety. My doctor says pregnant women have this, but it happens more to me. Mum says don't be silly, forget it, so I don't talk about it much.

ANDREA. I think of you all the time, I cuddle you. I imagine your feet, fingers and hands. It is so moving to feel you in me. I'm sure you will have dark hair like all my family and your father's.

LAURA. I think you will be blonde. Your father is. And my parents are fair. I am the only dark one. There's a lost great-grandfather somewhere who left me his genes. My mother insists that my hair darkened over the years.

ANDREA. I have three pieces of good news.
First: no sickness for a week. Second:
Granny Clara's sister came yesterday
from Mercedes and said you are a girl,
and she is never wrong. Third: people
already give me their seat on the train.
Thanks, Laura! Such privilege makes
me feel like a queen.

PS: I found a part time job.

LAURA. Your father and my mother are
getting on my nerves telling me to stop
working, but I can't think of myself at
home all day. I'd die. You've got a hy-
peractive mother. I must have got it
from all the moving.

ANDREA. It is so hot. I've got a week off in
March and Dad wants us to go to Córdoba. I hope the doctor approves because I'll be in my seventh month. Dad
is painting our portraits on the quiet. I
saw him by chance this morning and he

will be flattering. I won't say I saw it so
it stays a surprise.

LAURA. Ximena, my best friend, gave me a
book of proverbs. The first I read was
by a native Indian group. It touched me
so I could not stop crying until I had
written it for you: 'When a child is born
the father shows him the world and the
mother embraces him to show that he is
the world.'

ANDREA. I was looking at carry-cots, and
though I am betting on pink, I'll buy a
white one.

PS: Can you believe it, father bought
you a Boca squad shirt!

LAURA. Boca won and it makes me happy. I
didn't tell you, and even if my parents
don't like it, I'm a real Boca fan.

ANDREA. Dad is very nervous and won't tell
me why. Today he suggested we bring
forward the holiday. I suppose he is like

that because he is going to be a father.
Men get more scared than we do as the
time gets closer. That's what my mother
says, and she had five children.

LAURA. Two victories. One, Dad agrees to
be with us when you are born. I am
relieved not to be alone. Second: he
agrees to your name. It slipped out
when we were looking at the screen, I
looked at him and we giggled. Anyway,
I wasn't going to give up that easily.
Laura, the five letters are all yours, with
all the strength of its brilliance. Laura, I
love you. I am happy.

ANDREA. Sorry I haven't written for a week.
We've had a military coup. There's a lot
of trouble. Your granny is worried
about me going to university. Your Dad
had to leave suddenly for Salta because
of problems in the Students' Union. He
asked me to go alone to Córdoba and
we'll meet at the bus terminal. He

didn't sleep much these days, and his asthma's back. He was sweating too much. He left at five in the morning, there was not much light and I pretended to be asleep, I've always hated partings. He kissed my belly, my eyes, kissed me all over and stood in the room for some time. He left us the portrait on the bed, signed 'I love you'. That filled me with sadness. How strange. I rubbed my face in his pillow to smell his scent.

LAURA. After you're born, I am going to write down every detail, so that when you are grown up I can help you. Can you believe my mother doesn't remember anything and can't explain it?

ANDREA. I have milk in my nipples; it's called colostrum. It's good to know we are stocking the pantry. Buenos Aires is so strange—it frightens me. All I want now is to get to Córdoba. Dad called today in a great hurry and sent us kisses.

LAURA. When I eat chocolate you jump like a little rabbit. It makes you happy. Like it does me eating it. Our hearts beat together and in harmony.

ANDREA. I get nervous when you stop moving and worry that something's wrong, but if I eat a chocolate you immediately get going. You're a fatty at heart, like your mother!

LAURA. I love you.

ANDREA. I love you more than myself; I love you madly.

LAURA. I feel you.

ANDREA. I can see you barefoot, running naked.

LAURA. Dawn embraces us, the fading moon touches me.

ANDREA. I am in love with you and you make me fall in love with you.

LAURA. And I am happy.

ANDREA. Happy.

LAURA. The doctor says you are well
formed. You just have to grow and so
must I. Dad is in doubt again about
being with me. I'll panic. If he doesn't
come, I'll ask Ximena.

ANDREA. Everything was on time. Green
wallpaper in your room and I bought
your cot. Your grannies are in a frenzy
of knitting; they are embroidering your
sheets. And I have your bag ready just
in case you decide to give us a surprise.
Two months and you'll be here.

LAURA. I'm betting on life. A child is a bet
on life. That's what matters now.

ANDREA. Dad was very strange. He called
early and suggested we don't go to Córdoba, but I won't have that. We are
going there tonight . . . and we'll be
having breakfast together at the station.

Just a few hours feel like years. I'll write
to you there.

The light goes out over Andrea. She exits.

LAURA. I had a check yesterday, and I
heard your heartbeat, it was regular,
rhythmic, with mine. I cried a little. A
person at the clinic mistook me for
somebody else. She called me Andrea
. . . and was very overcome . . . Her eyes
filled with tears. I didn't understand
what was going on. My husband was in
a hurry and took me to the car, but I
felt she had more to tell me. Anyway, all
that matters now is you.

(*Short silence on stage. Laura looks to where
Andrea was sitting*)

I couldn't sleep last night, even though
I practiced all the relaxation I was
taught on the course. I couldn't stop
thinking of the face of that nurse . . . or
maybe doctor. I feel my chest closing
and I am filled with anxiety.

(*Short silence*)

Two days now and I can't stop thinking
of that woman. I think I'll go to see her.

(*Silence*)

I worked up courage and went to the
clinic to find that woman. She is a doctor, a specialist in contagious diseases.
Patricia. When she saw me she shook all
over again. When she calmed down she
offered me coffee and the conversation
was a monologue, full of words that hit
me strangely, I was a bit shaken, because her words sounded familiar, even
the way she moved her hands . . . She
kept walking around my chair. She
talked of somebody she had met a long
time ago and thought that I might be
her daughter Laura. That's the name
she gave and said she had been at the
birth, to help, when she was a medical
student. Then she stopped, stared at
me, and burst into tears. She hugged

me, kissed me . . . Apologized, and suddenly I felt very small again.

(*Silence*)

Laura . . . like my Laura . . . I feel faint, short of air.

The lights go out. In the darkness a spot shines centre stage on a space like a basement. Andrea, looking dishevelled, sits on the floor.

ANDREA. It's so hot here, I can hardly breathe. The good news vanished with the pens, but I am not going to stop our chats and I am going to memorize every word until I can write them down when they let me out. They say that us pregnant women will be taken to have our babies outside of here; then they release the babies. I know nothing of your father. They don't talk nicely about him, nor about me, but don't listen to them. I sing to you as much as possible, though my voice is croaking.

The pain doesn't let me sleep.

Lights up, showing Laura.

LAURA. Patricia is a ghost, I can't get her out of my thoughts. Her face, her scent. It's as if I knew her. I couldn't tell anybody about her.

ANDREA. I felt better today, they are not questioning me so much. There are other pregnant women here and we all try to talk just about you little people. One of them is lovely Patricia. She's a medical student who helps us with our exercises.

LAURA. Patricia calls me all the time and I can't answer. I'm in a bad mood, don't sleep much, and the pain in the chest won't go away. I mentioned a bit to Mum and she went pale and came at me with all that about not talking to strangers . . . and blah blah. I can't stop thinking about the coincidences.

ANDREA. I'm terrified. Claudia, one of the
girls who was pregnant, had her baby
yesterday. A boy. Pablo. She did not go
to any hospital and delivered him here,
and then he was taken away from her.
They said they were giving him to her
mother. My God! I worry that Mum is
never at home and she might not know
that she has to go and fetch you, and
she'll be desperate. She won't know the
address . . . Laura, I don't want you to
leave.

LAURA. I feel better. It helped to unplug
the phone. I feel less pain in my chest.
Your room is a delight. Your cot is fit
for a queen.

ANDREA. Today I was told that your father
was arrested at a friend's house in Salta
just as he was leaving for Córdoba. He's
alive. He's alive and I miss him very
much.

LAURA. The old man knows everything.
Mum told him. He came to question me.
I was angry, he very angry. I ignored
him. He wouldn't let go. Quite apart
from the silence and the squabble, I
know there is something I don't know.

ANDREA. I have lost my sense of time and
space. I can't remember how many days
I've been here. I tried to sing to you but
can't. I am very angry. I don't know why
this is happening to me. I don't understand, I don't know what they are talking about. I don't understand their
language.

I'm afraid. You cheer me with your little
kicks. Kick, Laura, please kick! The
girls look after me. Claudia can't stop
crying and touches our stomachs. I've
begun to pray. You are my favourite
star, my north, my sun, my everything.
I know God will have pity on us and a
miracle will happen.

LAURA. Patricia brought me this box. (*She puts it on the writing table*) She told me to look at the photos, baby clothes and a book written for me. And I don't know why I don't tell her to piss off. (*She opens the box slowly*) My chest hurts. (*She takes out the exercise book and opens it*)

'Hello son, or daughter: The written word, I think, suits me better to speak my feelings. I am usually quiet and shy, you will soon see, but this moment is so big I think I must be as talkative as possible. Oh, we've had your name for ages, Juan if you're a boy, Laura if you are lucky to be the stronger sex. And as I know about these things . . . I am sure you are Laura.'

ANDREA. Laura, I speak to you, I remember you to write to you, and I write to remember myself. If God Almighty will allow it, my darling little one, light of my eyes that are now blind from so

much darkness, I know you will not
have your first night in your green
room or your white clothes, but you will
have my nipples to heal you. You will
go from me, through me, to an eternity
of two, mother and daughter. I will
have your taste of milk, of salt and sea
in the mornings.

The pains are coming more quickly
now . . . I feel so bad about partings . . .
You will give me the joy of being a
mother and nobody can take that from
me and you will be my light now and
for ever. One more heave and you will
be mine. I love you more than myself, I
love you madly.

(*She calls*) Patricia . . . !

Help me, Patricia.

You come into my heart. I bless you,
smell you, lick you and hold you. Eternity in an instant, my sun in this hole.
(*Pushing*) Nobody will erase your name,

Laura, daughter of Andrea and Marcos,
not guilty, in love, human. Lauraaa!
(*Baby cries.*)

LAURA (*her call mixes with the shout of her
mother and the baby's crying*). Mother!

(*Light out over Andrea.*) I am me. One
can't be so blind or so deaf not to see or
hear, nor so dumb not to speak truths,
one can't be so alone from aloneness.

ANDREA (*speaking softly. Alone. She walks and
the light comes up*). You were born to look
like me, like my first photographs. With
black, very black hair, and dark eyes
like your father's. You stuck to my
breast and were silent. Not a peep, sure
of yourself you felt your way. You were
born Taurus, on 10 May 1976. (*She sings
the first lines of 'Necesito', a popular song,
as a lullaby*) I love you from deep inside,
with my heart I open your wings. I em-
brace you and surround you in your
world as we create a new one. I feel you

large, open. I touch your skin, your salt,
your eyes, your light, your smell, and
our senses dance for joy that the miracle is possible even in the shadows,
where you are the Light.

LAURA. I wonder how many times I will
have your little hand in mine.

ANDREA. I hold your hand 500 times in
mine. I kiss you all over, I include you
in my heart and like magic I find a
mole in the middle of your chest, and
that is my signature for ever.

LAURA (*starts panting*). You are coming, little one. You are coming, Laura, my
Laura.

The light goes down slowly. A baby cries.

Notes

1 Marc Augé, *Non-Lieux, Introduction à une anthropologie de la surmodernité* (Paris: Edition de Seuil, 1992). English translation: *Non-Places: Introduction to an Anthropology of Supermodernity* (John Howe trans.) (London: Verso, 2009).

2 Simon Sebag Montefiore, *Stalin: The Court of the Red Tsar* (London: Weidenfeld & Nicolson, 2003), p. 203.

3 Timothy Snyder, 'Holocaust: The Ignored Reality' [available at: www.eurozine.com], 2009.

4 Linda Melvern, *Conspiracy to Murder: The Rwanda Genocide* (London: Verso, 2006).

5 Enrique Dussel, 'Eurocentrism and Modernity', *Boundary* 2(20) (1993): 65–76.

6 Cecilia Vicuña, 'An Introduction to Mestizo Poetics', in Cecilia Vicuña and Ernesto Livon-Grosman (eds), *The Oxford Book of Latin American Poetry* (Oxford: Oxford University Press, 2009), pp. xix–xxxii. The quote is from p. xx.

7 Benjamín Prado, '¿Será Usted un niño robado por el franquismo?' ('Might you be a Child Stolen in Franco's Time?'), *El País*, 16 January 2009; Miguel Ángel Rodríguez Arias and Ricard Vinyes Ribes, *El caso de los niños perdidos del franquismo: crimen contra la humanidad* ('The Case of the Children Lost Under Franco: A Crime against Humanity') (Barcelona: Editorial Debolsillo, 2008).

8 Antonio Machado, 'Mala gente que camina y va apestando la tierra' ('Bad people who Walk and go Poisoning the Earth') in *Soledades, Galerías, Otros poemas* (Barcelona: Editorial Labor, 1975), p. 65. English translation: *Solitudes, Galleries and Other Poems* (Richard L. Predmore trans.) (Durham: Duke Univeristy Press, 1987).

9 Benjamín Prado, *Mala gente que camina* ('Bad People who Walk') (Madrid: Alfaguara, 2006).

10 Robin Blackburn, *The Overthrow of Colonial Slavery, 1776–1848* (London: Verso, 1988).

11 Alex Haley, *Roots: The Saga of an American Family* (New York: Doubleday, 1976).

12 Toni Morrison made her debut as a novelist in 1970. Among her best-known novels are *The Bluest Eye* (1970), *Song of Solomon* (1977) and *Beloved* (1987), for which she was awarded the Pulitzer Prize for Fiction in 1988. She won the Nobel Prize for Literature in 1993.

13 Erskine Caldwell is best known for *Tobacco Road* (1932) and *God's Little Acre* (1933).

14 Ana Miranda, *Boca do Inferno* (Lisbon: Dom Quixote, 1990). English translation: *Bay of All Saints and Every Conceivable Sin* (Giovanni Pontiero trans.) (London: Viking, 1992).

15 Antônio Olinto, *A Casa da Água* (Rio de Janeiro: Ed. Bloch, 1969). English translation: *The Water House* (Dorothy Healy trans.) (London: Rex Collings, 1970).

16 Isabel Fonseca, *Bury me Standing: the Gypsies and Their Journey* (New York: Alfred Knopf, 1995).

17 Musa Moris Farhi, *Children of the Rainbow* (London: Saqi Books, 1999).

18 Tania Buri in *Voices—Unabridged*: e-magazine on Women and Human Rights Worldwide [available at: www.voices-unabridged.net/article.php?id_article=-175&numero=12], 18 April 2007.

19 (Rosa) Graciela (Castagnola) Fernández Meijide, *La historia íntima de los derechos humanos en la Argentina* ('The Intimate History of Human Rights in Argentina'). (Buenos Aires: Sudamericana, 2007). In this book, Fernández Meijide queries the inflated number of 30,000 victims projected from the 9,000 victims reported by the Nunca Más (Never Again) Commission set up by President Raúl Alfonsín in 1984. A teacher by profession and founder of the Permanent Assembly of Human Rights (APDH), Fernández Meijide was an elected national deputy and national senator in the 1990s. She dedicated her book to the memory of her son Pablo, who disappeared in October 1976.

20 Attributed alternatively to General Jorge Rafael Videla and to General Alcides López Aufranc at a meeting of heads of armies in Montevideo in the mid-1970s. The attributions were later denied by spokespersons of both.

21 Horacio Verbitsky, *El vuelo*: *'una forma cristiana de muerte', confesiones de un oficial de la Armada* (Buenos Aires: Planeta, 1995). English translation: *The Flight: Confessions of an Argentine Dirty Warrior* (Esther Allen trans.) (New York: New Press, 1996). This book is considered instrumental in President Néstor Kirchner's decision to overturn the pardons that benefited the military in the 1980s and early 1990s.

22 Marguerite Feitlowitz, *A Lexicon of Terror*: *Argentina and the Legacies of Torture* (Oxford: Oxford University Press, 1998).

23 Horacio Verbitsky, *Doble juego*: *la Argentina Católica y Militar* ('Double Game: Catholic and Military Argentina') (Buenos Aires: Sudamericana, 2006).

24 This explanation was given to two editors of the English-language *Buenos Aires
   Herald* in September 1976 by the information minister, Captain (later Admiral)
   Carlos Carpintero, who objected to the
   coverage of the 'disappeared' by the
   Herald.

25 Sara Méndez, 'La coordinación represiva
   en el Cono sur a través de sus víctimas'
   ('Coordinated Repression in the South-
   ern Cone by way of the Victims), in
   *Memorias de la violencia en Uruguay y Ar-
   gentina*: *Golpes, dictaduras, exilios,
   1973–2006* ('Memories of Violence in
   Uruguay and Argentina: Coups, Dictatorship, Exile, 1973–2006) (Eduardo Rey
   Tristán ed.) (Santiago: Universidade de
   Santiago de Compostela, 2007), pp.
   133–52. The quote is from p. 143. Translation mine.

26 Patricia Marchak, *God's Assassins*: *State Ter-
   rorism in Argentina in the 1970s*. (Montreal:
   McGill-Queen's University Press, 1999).

27 Gitta Sereny, *The German Trauma*: *Experi-*

ences and Reflections 1938–1999 (London: Penguin, 2002).

28 Jorge Volnovich, 'El torno y la vara' ('The Turn-table and the Cane'), in *Palabra y Persona* 6(6–7) (July 2009): 165–90.

29 Isaac Bashevis Singer, 'The Colony', in *A Friend of Kafka and Other Stories* (New York: Farrar, Straus and Giroux, 1970), pp. 205–18.

30 Simha Sneh, interview with Andrew Graham-Yooll, Buenos Aires, 19 December 1994.

31 Argentine National Commission on the Disappeared, *Nunca Más: Report of the Argentine National Commission on the Disappeared* (Ronald Dworkin introd.) (New York: Farrar, Straus and Giroux, in association with *Index on Censorship*, 1986).

32 Rita Arditti, *Searching for Life: The Grandmothers of the Plaza de Mayo and the Disappeared Children of Argentina* (Berkeley and Los Angeles: University of California Press, 1999).

33 Asociación de Abuelas de Plaza de Mayo, *Teatro x la Identidad*: *obras de teatro del Ciclo 2001* ('Theatre of Identity: Plays of the 2001 Cycle') (Buenos Aires: Asociación Abuelas de Plaza de Mayo, 2001).

34 On 23 June 2003, the Arcola Theatre, London, staged three short plays from the series 'Theatre for Identity': *The Interview* by Bruno Luciani; *A Propos of Doubt* by Patricia Zangaro; *In Labour* by Marta Betoldi.

35 Claudia Carlotto, *Comisión Nacional por el Derecho a la Identidad (CoNaDI)*, *El trabajo del Estado en la recuperación de la identidad de jóvenes apropiados en la última dictadura militar* ('The Work by the State for the Recovery of the Identity of Young People Appropriated During the Last Military Dictatorship') (Buenos Aires: CoNaDI, 2007).

36 Guillermo Wulff (comp.), *Las abuelas y la genética, el aporte de la ciencia en la búsqueda de chicos desaparecidos* ('Grandmothers and Genetics, Scientific Contribution to the Search for Disappeared

Children') (Buenos Aires: Asociación Abuelas de Plaza de Mayo and Church World Service, 2008); Abel Madariaga (ed.), *Derecho a la identidad y persecución de crímenes de lesa humandad* ('Right to Identity and Pursuit of Crimes against Humanity) (Buenos Aires: Asociación Abuelas de Plaza de Mayo, 2008).

37 Alicia Lo Giúdice (comp.), *Centro de Atención por el Derecho a la Identidad de Abuelas de Plaza de Mayo. Psicoanálisis: identidad y transmisión* (Centre for Attention for the Right of Identity of the Grandmothers of Plaza de Mayo. Psychoanalisis: Identity and Transmission) (Buenos Aires: Asociación Abuelas de Plaza de Mayo and Department of Justice, the Government of Basque, 2008).

38 Delia Maunás, *Boris Spivacow*, *Memoria de un sueño argentine* (Boris Spivacow, Memoir of an Argentine Dream) (Buenos Aires: Colihue, 1995); Horacio González and Judith Gociol, *Más libros para más. Colecciones del Centro Editor de Amércial Latina* (More Books for More. Collections of the Centro Editor de América Latina)

(Buenos Aires: Ediciones Biblioteca Nacional, 2008).

While book-burning in Argentina was frequent during the military dictatorship as a way of stamping out 'subversive' ideas and elements, the most notorious case was the destruction in the provinces of Córdoba and Buenos Aires of the imprint Centro Editor de América Latina (CEAL), led by the late Boris Spivacow (1915–94). Spivacow, a writer and later a publisher, was the founder of the National University of Buenos Aires imprint, Eudeba, in June 1958, and was sacked after the military coup in June 1966. He then started CEAL, which was closed after the coup in 1976 and its entire stock burned. Another imprint whose stock was seized in 1976 was the Editorial Siglo XXI. The 700-page catalogue of the publications of CEAL and recollections of the staff was compiled by the National Library of Argentina under its director Horacio González.

39 A notorious detention camp first identified in the report *Never Again*.—Ed.

40 Military barracks.—Ed.

41 A notorious detention centre, later used in a film, *Garage Olimpo* (1999).—Ed.

42 The drums are traditionally used in the *murgas*, popular musical theatre played during carnival, and have been adopted in most political demos.—Ed.

INDEX
ON CENSORSHIP

Index on Censorship is Britain's leading organization
promoting freedom of expression. Our award-winning
magazine and website provide a window for original,
challenging and intelligent writing on this vital issue
around the world. Our international projects in media,
arts and education put our philosophy into action.

For information and enquiries go to
www.indexoncensorship.org,
or email enquiries@indexoncensorship.org

To subscribe to Index on Censorship, or find stockists in your
area, go to http://www.indexoncensorship.org/getyourcopy
or phone
(+44) 20 7017 5544 for the United Kingdom
or (+1) 518 537 4700 in the United States

www.indexoncensorship.org